The POWER of ONE

2006-7 NMI
MISSION EDUCATION RESOURCES

✽ ✽ ✽

BOOKS

EIGHT STEPS FROM THE EDGE OF HELL
From Addiction to Ministry in Ukraine
by Sherry Pinson

EVERY FULL-MOON NIGHT
Life Lessons from Missionary Kids
by Dean Nelson

GLIMPSES OF GRACE
Mission Stories from Bolivia
by Randy Bynum

THE POWER OF ONE
Compassion as a Lifestyle
by Ellen Decker

SHOULD I KISS OR SHAKE HANDS?
Surviving in Another Culture
by Pat Stockett Johnston

SHOUTS AT SUNRISE
The Abduction and Rescue of Don Cox
by Keith Schwanz

✽ ✽ ✽

ADULT MISSION EDUCATION RESOURCE BOOK

MISSION FAMILIES
Editors: Wes Eby and Rosanne Bolerjack

The POWER of ONE

COMPASSION AS A LIFESTYLE

Ellen DECKER

Nazarene Publishing House
Kansas City, Missouri

DEDICATION

To all those who, like Jesus, live
compassion as a lifestyle

CONTENTS

ELLEN GAILEY DECKER

is an ordained elder in the Church of the Nazarene. She has served in a variety of pastoral, missions, and communication roles at the local, district, and general church levels. Rev. Decker has preached in states across the Eastern Region. An MK (missionary kid) from Swaziland, Africa, Ellen has lived on three continents and traveled to almost 30 countries. She and her husband, Hank, have three sons —Ryan, Jason, and Kevin. Their favorite family activity is trekking together in Africa.

Ellen has been published in *Today's Christian Woman*, *Virtue*, *World Mission*, *Holiness Today*, *Come Ye Apart/Reflecting God*, and various NMI publications. Since 1999 she has written and edited publications for Nazarene Compassionate Ministries, International. She is the founding editor of *Nazarene Compassionate Ministries* magazine.

Ellen's life verse is Acts 20:24: "I consider my life worth nothing to me, if only I may finish the race and complete the task the Lord Jesus has given me—the task of testifying to the gospel of God's grace."

FOREWORD

Elijah stood alone against the prophets of Baal. Jesus used one lad's tiny lunch to feed thousands. The grand biblical God-moments include an obedient, surprised human partner. We can do nothing without God's majestic intervention. God respects our freedom and will do nothing without us. We each have the joyous honor and the frightening privilege of being partners with God. We each have *the power of one* to make a compassionate difference!

The Power of One is a magnificent book for pastors and mission leaders who want to be inspired and changed. This is also a powerful tool for new believers and lifelong saints who yearn to grow in their compassion-stewardship of time, talent, and money.

Ellen Decker is not a researcher developing a theoretical topic. She is a passionate missional practitioner who shares from her heart what she is learning about God's love and mission.

Nazarene Compassionate Ministry's simple formula of

- unconditional assistance and
- intentional evangelism
- is yielding eternal results

from Armenia to Zambia. *The Power of One* is a celebration of compassionate ministries, opening the doors for the Church of the Nazarene to enter new world areas.

This book is the story of how
- one person
- with God
- can make an eternal difference.

Discover again that compassion is not a peripheral act or an optional offering, but a lifestyle—the lifestyle of Jesus.

Jerry D. Porter
General Superintendent
Church of the Nazarene

ACKNOWLEDGMENTS

I gratefully acknowledge those who have contributed to this book:

- Bob Prescott, former NCM administrative director, graciously took time from a demanding schedule to discuss the book's stories with me and to share his knowledge of the global compassionate ministries of the Church of the Nazarene. Bob also lent his considerable Spanish expertise, translating information received from El Salvador, Peru, and Guatemala.
- Other NCM directors, past and present, Steve Weber, Gustavo Crocker, and Larry Bollinger —your work has made a global difference.
- The people whose names are in this book— your compassionate lifestyles made these stories possible, and the world is profoundly grateful.
- All NCM volunteers and employees worldwide—may God bless you for leading the way with Christlikeness.
- Bethany Wright for NCM, Inc., reports; Jeannette Brubaker and Rev. Lynn Shaw for their services; and Wes Eby, my editor, for encouragement on the journey.
- My family—Hank, Ryan, Jason, and Kevin— without your love and support this book would still be a dream. "Siyabonga Kakhulu, guys!"

- My Lord and Savior, Jesus Christ, my audience of One—to You I owe all.

Ellen Decker

PROLOGUE

A funny thing happened on the way to the African interior in 2003 when our family stopped at a restaurant off the beaten track. I struck up a conversation with a gentleman in the buffet line, and discovered that I just happened to be standing next to a Nazarene who lived hundreds of miles away from where we were. Bivocational pastor Dr. Ruston Mhlongo and his wife, Audrey, were on their way to facilitate, without pay, three "Life Skills" AIDS workshops for teachers in South Africa. These gentle saints of God had given up their vacations for the past five years to teach these AIDS seminars.

It greatly encourages and humbles us to hear about global disciples of Christ like the Mhlongos who are quietly choosing compassion as a lifestyle. As earthquakes, floods, drought, volcanic eruptions, fires, disease, and hunger devastate people in every world region, we want to help. Yet, sometimes we wonder if we can really make a difference. Compassionate individuals inspire us because their choice of sacrificial living authenticates that one person has the power to make a profound difference in a hurting world.

NAZARENES DON'T JUST FEEL SYMPATHY FOR THE WORLD'S MISERY; WE TAKE ACTION TO ALLEVIATE IT.

As a child in Africa I learned the Zulu word for compassion: *umhawu,* meaning "oneness." Its more specific meaning is translated "understanding on behalf of another." The Zulus would say, "We imagine what it is like to live in someone else's skin."

Webster defines compassion as "sympathetic feelings of another's distress *along with the desire to alleviate it*" (emphasis added).

Nazarenes don't just feel sympathy for the world's misery; we take action to alleviate it. From 1992 to 2005, 29 of the 58 new world areas for the work of the Church of the Nazarene were entered through compassionate ministries, by individuals who imagined what it is like to live in someone else's suffering.

The church desperately needs individuals who are God-inspired to understand on behalf of another, who empathize with what it is like to live in someone else's skin, who believe in the *power of one* to alleviate suffering. The stories in this book are about some of those who have dared to believe.

ONE MAKES A DIFFERENCE

CENY

When Ceny woke up, she was tingling with excitement. Christmas had arrived, and to a child in the Philippines, Christmas was the most important day of the year. She ran quickly to look at her old sock hanging by the window. Her face fell. It was empty. Again.

Growing up with six brothers and two sisters in a destitute family in the Philippines, Ceny is familiar with disappointment. Basic necessities, such as clothing, came only once a year, if at all. As an adult looking for better economic prospects, Ceny traveled to Bangkok, Thailand, to work first for a private trading company and then with the Christian and Missionary Alliance refugee work. During this time she met and married Tomo Hirahara from Japan. In 1995 they went to the Philippines to study at Asia-Pacific Nazarene Theological Seminary, where each received a master of divinity. They have been serving as Nazarene missionaries in Thailand since 1999.

Ceny soon realized God was calling her to a unique ministry. "Growing up in poverty prepared me to love the many who are poor and suffering in Thailand," Ceny says. "God gave me a deep love for the Thai people, and my heart beat to do more than just know about their pain. I wanted to reach out and make a difference in their lives. Sawat Hahom, Thailand District superintendent, mentioned the possibility of a ministry to people with AIDS. God reminded me of Jeremiah 1:4-8, especially verses 7b-8: "'You must go to everyone I send you to and say whatever I command you. Do not be afraid of them, for I am with you and will rescue you,' declares the LORD."

This was the birth of a new ministry for Ceny as coordinator of New Life for Thai, so named in the hope that patients suffering from HIV/AIDS will find new life in Christ. Establishing good relationships with medical personnel and government agencies is critical for a Christian group in a Buddhist country. (New Life for Thai now has working relationships with nine health centers, local NGOs [nongovernmental organizations], and some government agencies on AIDS.)

Holding seminars that inform church members about AIDS is also important because of misconceptions and stigma. Church members want to show love and compassion, but there are also grave concerns about how contagious AIDS is. Would people come to the church if they knew there were attendees with AIDS?

Gradually a group of volunteers came together, including Suvit Amonkulsawat who resigned his job to join the ministry as a project staff member. Volunteers take extensive training through various agencies and national AIDS seminars. They study nutri-

New Life for Thai team. Ceny Hirahara is second from left in front.

tion, counseling AIDS patients, use of traditional and herbal medicines, project administration, and a comprehensive understanding of the disease itself.

"Working in the Thai culture can be challenging," states Ceny. "*Thiaw geng* refers to someone who wants to have sex with prostitutes. It has the same meaning as 'playboy.' Many men who work in Bangkok get infected with HIV and then take it home to their wives. Tragically, many wives only discover they are infected when they have blood tests for pregnancy."

Sunni (not her real name) is one woman who discovered she had AIDS when she was pregnant. Here is her story:

I am 37 years old. I married a good man who loved me and our one son. When he died in an accident, I had to work in a factory for many years.

Then I met a man, and we got married. I was so happy to have a house to live in. After about three months I got pregnant and went to the doctor. I was very surprised to find out I had AIDS from my husband. Things quickly got worse. He lost his job as a carpenter. He gambled away his money and drank a lot. I tried to earn money by selling desserts, but when my husband began to show his AIDS symptoms, people stopped buying them. The only good thing was that my son was born without AIDS.

I was desperate. Our house was taken away. I had no money to pay rent, and they turned off our utilities. I had no rice for my children. I cried a lot and felt hopeless. I wanted to kill myself and my children too. Then one day I met Ceny and Rev. Hahom. I had opportunity to hear the story about God, and saw a movie about Him (*JESUS* film). I realized I am a sinner and need a Redeemer. I opened the door of my life and asked God to come into my heart. God has given me strength to live again.

THE MESSAGE OF HOLINESS OF THE CHURCH OF THE NAZARENE IS THE BEST HOPE FOR AIDS PATIENTS.

Now I want to tell AIDS patients that there is life in our souls. We are people, just like others. We do not have to be afraid. We do not have to think of ourselves as dirty or worthless because we are poor and sick. We are people of value and can be useful and help others. Best of all, we do not have to be lonely. All because of God's love for us.

Ceny is convinced that the message of holiness of the Church of the Nazarene is the best hope for AIDS patients. "Letting them see Christ in us as we eat with them, laugh with them, and hug them," she says, "shows them the deep love God has even in the midst of their despair and loneliness."

One time Ceny and another team member helped get Ana (not her real name) to the hospital. "In the waiting room Ana's four-year-old daughter just kept looking at me with her round, scared eyes," Ceny says. "The grandmother was exhausted, trying to take care of both her granddaughter and Ana. The relatives don't visit or help because Ana has AIDS."

Ana died a few weeks later, but not before she found peace with God. The attending nurse said, "I have never seen someone so peaceful." New Life for Thai was invited to hold a Christian funeral service in the Buddhist temple area before Ana's cremation.

"Because caregiving involves personal services, such as buying and preparing food, giving medicine, and accompanying patients to the hospital, a close relationship is established," Ceny says. "So when a patient dies, we grieve too. We have lost a friend and often a new sister in Christ."

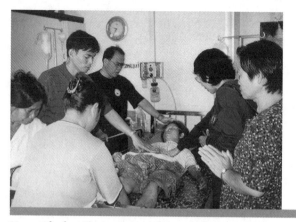
New Life for Thai praying for an AIDS patient

New Life for Thai especially tries to reach out to the children, often shunned by playmates, with special events like trips to the zoo. Each year they throw a Christmas party to celebrate the love of God and to give the patients a gift—the only gift many of the kids receive. A Japanese youth team assisted with the first party in 2002. At the holiday festivity the next year, three AIDS patients prayed to receive Christ. "It's critical for us to establish a friendship with them," says Ceny. "When they see we genuinely care and that we are in this for the long haul, they respond to that love."

New Life for Thai also helps AIDS patients become self-supporting. Several patients make beautiful handwoven bags to sell. One patient, Cindy (not her real name), is making handmade, traditional Thai cards. Cindy was saved when a New Life for Thai volunteer presented the gospel to her using an EvangeCube. Cindy, age 26, has two children. The proceeds from her cards go to help her handicapped child and to buy milk for her baby, so she won't get AIDS from breastfeeding.

"This ministry can be intense, but it is deeply rewarding," says Ceny. "Thanks to the efforts of Rev. Hahom, Mr. Amonkulsawat, and our volunteers, we are seeing God move in incredible ways as He loves the AIDS patients through us."

People's lives are being changed as they receive hope in Christ because Ceny Hirahara believed she could make a difference.

Amber

What started as a crooked smile for four-year-old Amber Westman developed into total deafness in her left ear. It didn't take long for the diagnosis: a rare, inoperable brain tumor. Amber was given a maximum of eight months to live; yet she baffled doctors by continuing to survive for several years. Despite being so ill herself, Amber's compassionate heart enjoyed reaching out to people, and she would often make crafts and food for those who were hurting.

One day Amber saw her grandmother and some friends knitting little sweaters. She seemed pleased when her grandmother told her they were to protect babies in Africa from the cold winter nights.

As Amber lost her hair and steroids left her swollen, she grew more thoughtful and quiet. One day she asked her grandmother to take all her toys

LuAnn is blind, but her disability doesn't slow down this talented, highly motivated young lady.

out of her closet. Then she looked at her grandmother and said quietly, "I want my toys to be sold and the money given to help those babies in Africa." Her grandmother agreed, telling Amber they would work on it together.

Amber never made it to the yard sale. But her grandmother kept her promise by selling Amber's toys and sending a check for $100 to Nazarene Compassionate Ministries (NCM). The money was used to help provide orphaned AIDS babies with blankets. One makes a difference!

LuAnn

LuAnn Howe is a remarkable and gifted young lady. She plays four instruments and sings in three languages. An honor student, she writes her own songs and sets up her own sound system when performing. She sings for senior citizen's groups, children's ministries, camps, and nursing homes. LuAnn is blind, but her disability doesn't slow down this talented, highly motivated young lady.

LuAnn held a concert at the Macungie Church of the Nazarene in Pennsylvania to benefit NCM. Her concert included 19 songs. Three were her own compositions, and some were in Spanish and German. The benefit raised $1,253 for the NCM fund. One makes a difference!

LuAnn Howe

KRISTI

Cancer! This was not in Kristi Nolan's plans. Yet in spite of the devastating news, Kristi, a beautiful high school junior, continued to live compassion as a lifestyle. She took in treats for the other kids on the cancer ward, and she kept knitting her blankets. Kristi, along with several ladies in the Lakeview, Ohio, Nazarene church, had caught a vision of making blankets for babies in Albania when missionaries Steve and Rachael Beiler had described the severe winters there.

Kristi Nolan

Until she died in 2002, Kristi was still asking her nurses, "Do you know Jesus?"

"Kristi had an incredible testimony," her pastor, Rev. Glen Freshour, says. "She simply loved people with an amazing compassion. Doctors and nurses traveled over 80 miles to attend her funeral."

Two large boxes of blankets and booties—invested with love, time, and energy—were sent to Albania and distributed through a village health-care project. Kristi's mother describes how hard it was to let her daughter's blankets go: "I held them to my heart awhile and cried. She had just completed her second blanket a few days before she died. But I knew she would want me to send them, because that's the kind of girl our Kristi was—always thinking of others." Yes, one makes a difference!

ONE PLUS ONE

Dr. Phineas Bresee, one of the principal founders of the Church of the Nazarene, said: "Let the poor be fed and clothed; let us pour out our substances for this purpose; but let us keep heaven open, that they may receive the unspeakable gift of His love, in the transforming power of the Holy Ghost."*

Compassion, plus evangelism, is the hallmark of the holiness people called Nazarenes.

EL SALVADOR

"Who are you? Why are you here? We don't know you people," said the old man. The years of sun and hard labor in the fields showed on his face and stooped body. His grandson stood at his side.

Ulyssis Solis, chairman of the NCM committee responding to the massive earthquakes in El Salvador, looked up to see who was speaking to him. Rev. Solis explained to the man that the people needed help, and this was sufficient reason for the Nazarenes to come to their town, Llano Grande, to help.

The elderly man could not understand why total strangers would help. Rev. Solis took out his New Testament and read John 3:16: "For God so loved

---

The Quotable Bresee, compiled by Harold Ivan Smith (Kansas City: Beacon Hill Press of Kansas City, 1983), 168.

the world that He gave . . ." He shared with the man about this love that reaches out to people even before they know they need it, and even when they do not deserve it. Rev. Solis then asked the old man if he would like to experience God's love for himself.

"Si," he said with a nod. Rev. Solis led the grandfather in a simple prayer of repentance, confession, and faith in Jesus Christ. It seemed almost too easy. Yet Romans 10:13 says, "Everyone who calls on the name of the Lord will be saved." The old man put his bag of food on his head and walked off with his grandson.

This conversion happened while the church was responding to the 2001 earthquakes in El Salvador. The damage and destruction were unbelievable, especially in a residential area of San Salvador, which was buried in 25 feet of dirt. Twelve hundred people died, including eight Nazarenes. A local NYI president Fernando Melendez was away attending a ministerial class when the quake struck. His wife and three children were killed instantly as the avalanche of dirt buried their home—the day of his oldest son's 15th birthday. Today Fernando is faithfully serving two of the new preaching points that resulted from the disaster.

Churches all across the Mexico/Central America (MAC) Region quickly collected relief supplies and sent two truckloads and a cash offering to El Salvador. The regional office in Guatemala City sent $2,000 of NCM funds. All of these were used to meet immediate needs of the 4,000 Nazarenes affected by the disaster.

Distributing food to earthquake survivors in El Salvador

Fifty-five Nazarene families suffered major damage or total loss of their homes. NCM raised money, and Work and Witness (W&W) teams built 44 houses and repaired 11. The small cement houses with metal roofs cost an average of $2,000 for materials. Volunteers Bill Porter and Dean Hull spent several months in El Salvador coordinating the W&W teams. The Los Angeles District sent $20,000 to repair the most damaged church, San Salvador First Church. Six other damaged churches were repaired with W&W and NCM funds.

Humedica International, a relief agency in Germany, sent $95,000 for blankets and food. Victor Alfaro, pastor of the Uzulutan Nazarene Church, sent his people out into 14 rural communities to obtain the names of the 1,000 most vulnerable families (5,000 people). The entire community turned out to watch the food distribution by volunteer Nazarenes who all wore white T-shirts with *Iglesia del Nazareno* (Church of the Nazarene) on the front and *Dios es Amor* (God loves you) on the back.

COMPASSION AND EVANGELISM (ONE PLUS ONE) EQUALS A WINNING COMBINATION.

The Nazarene leadership in El Salvador gained a new vision for evangelizing their communities. Laypeople went out to lead preaching points and new missions, winning many people to the Lord. They started Bible studies and discipled converts from the *JESUS* film.

Remember the old man who prayed to receive Christ in Llano Grande? Two weeks later Rev. Solis and his 95 volunteers went back. When they arrived late in the day, there on the side of the road was the old man, grinning from ear-to-ear. Standing behind him were 13 people. When Rev. Solis asked him who they were, he answered, "My converts!" With no Bible, no church, no preacher, no Sunday School teacher, this dear old man had shared John 3:16 and what he was feeling in his heart. And 13 people believed his witness and were saved.

Two weeks later when it was time for the final distribution of food, the old man's new congregation had grown to 25 converts. Llano Grande now has a tree church with a member of the Uzulutan Nazarene church going every week to preach under the mango tree. Once again, extending help in time of crisis opened the doors for hope and belief in Jesus Christ. Compassion and evangelism (one plus one) equals a winning combination. Our leaders in El Salvador report a total of 16 new preaching points (8 of which are now organized churches) and 580 new converts from the results of compassion evangelism. God continues to build His Church, one plus one.

INDIA

Party time! Celebrations commemorating the 52nd Republic Day in western India were happening on January 26, 2001, when disaster struck. A severe earthquake sent shock waves through almost 8,000 villages. When the dust settled, more than 18,000 people were dead, an additional 166,000 were injured, and a million-plus homes were damaged or destroyed.

In response to this vast devastation, Nazarenes immediately began mobilizing resources. The district superintendent of Bombay arranged with the government of India for NCM to work in 19 villages near the Pakistan border. Within days of the disaster, two medical teams from Reynolds Memorial Hospital and the Lions Club in Washim (1,500 miles away) and Humedica International in Germany were on-site to assist. The teams, assisted by three dozen local volunteers, treated more than 2,500 people. Humedica and Heart to Heart International sent shipments of baby food, medical supplies, blankets, food, and Crisis Care Kits, which were distributed by the teams.

Most of the villagers had faced cyclones and severe drought for the previous two years, and they were extremely grateful for the help from Nazarene Compassionate Ministries. "It is very nice of the church to distribute relief material among all the affected people, irrespective of caste or religion," commented one man. The head of a village remarked, "We sense that there are so many people in other countries who can feel our suffering. Thank you very much for staying with us during this crisis and for your valuable counseling to the hurting." Arun Noah, director of Reynolds Memorial Hospital, said, "These are only two out of the many village leaders who thanked us. There were also hundreds of women with tears in their eyes that simply expressed their appreciation with folded hands and 'God bless you.'

"Because of the help we were able to give during this crisis," Dr. Noah reports, "people in this Hindu culture came to trust the Christians. They saw we genuinely cared and were ethically distributing the supplies. One man was so excited about the help his village received that he donated 4,000 square meters of land to encourage the beginning of an English school under the supervision of the Church of the Nazarene."

Today the Christian school enrolls over 150 students and has expanded to include high school grades. Humedica International provided funding for an additional six elementary schools built by Nazarenes, further enhancing the relationship with the

Dr. Arun Noah giving medical care

Dr. Noah treating earthquake victims

Hindu population. In addition, a Nazarene community health center that is servicing 15 villages with preventative health care was established in the area. Five preaching points began that are growing today with the help of the *JESUS* film. "We are so thankful for this rare opportunity to show compassion to the villagers," states Dr. Noah, "because it has awakened their understanding that Christianity is about loving others like Jesus does."

PERU

Fifty-two seconds changed the lives of thousands in southern Peru forever. In 2001 a massive earthquake left 180,000 people facing winter with no water, no food, and no shelter. Nazarenes attending general assembly at the time responded immediately with a generous offering of $4,000. NCM quickly gathered tents, blankets, food, clothing, Crisis Care Kits, medicines, tools, and building materials. In partnership with Heart to Heart and Federal Express, NCM sent an air shipment of urgently needed supplies.

Missionary Al Swain describes the arrival of the 15-ton shipment. "After 40 hours on the road, sometimes traveling over sections literally split in the middle from the quake, the trucks arrived safely. About 20 of us unloaded [humanitarian aid] and then held an impromptu thanksgiving service to God, NCM, and all the persons in local churches who sent these items!" An evangelical NGO in Peru, whose president is a Nazarene, also sent two truckloads of mattresses and other supplies.

"Our local people were impacted greatly by the generosity of people from other parts of the world," reports District Superintendent Santiago Bereche. "The fact that the givers didn't know them, but sent relief anyway, really opened the door to the hearts of the people of Peru." Luis Meza, NCM coordinator for South America, arranged for the *JESUS* film to be shown at relief distribution sites.

Quake victims' lives were changed as they witnessed Peruvian Nazarenes be living examples of Jesus. All other relief groups left the disaster area and slept in hotels, but the Nazarenes pitched tents and stayed with the homeless people. Fernando was one young man whose home was badly damaged. The local church responded in love by giving his family basic necessities and sharing Christ. "I wasted my life on drunkenness," Fernando testifies. "It impacted my family negatively. Now I have Jesus in my life, and it's so much better!"

Prior to the quake, it took the Church of the Nazarene 20 years to plant two churches in that area. Within 2 years after the quake there were five active churches with over 500 members and several new preaching points. Rev. Meza shares insight about the strategy used after the quake. "In times like this it is crucial that the church show the love of Christ in action. Compassion and evangelism is the best combination to reach the world for Christ."

Yes, one plus one is an effective formula!

ONE C*3*OUNTRY
AT A TIME

Nazarene Compassionate Ministries (NCM) has led the way for the Church of the Nazarene to enter dozens of new world areas with the gospel. Compassion is reaching the world for Christ—one country at a time.

ARMENIA

Several days after an earthquake in 1989 killed 35,000 people and buried its people in the rubble, an atheist teacher stumbled into the street in Gyumri, Armenia. In front of neighbors and rescue workers, she knelt in the middle of the road, raised her arms to heaven, and cried in a loud voice, "If there is a God, please hear me. If You save my daughter's life, I will believe and serve You." Within hours her daughter, Anahid, was pulled alive from the rubble.

NCM asked Habib Alajaji, pastor of the Glendale Church of the Nazarene in California, to go to Armenia to assess the damage. For three weeks Dr. Alajaji traveled to three towns and preached nearly every day. Many came to the Lord, hungry for the gospel after their lives had been shattered. Many had lost their hands, arms, or legs. Even more had lost their loved ones, their homes, and all their possessions.

Pastor Habib met Anahid. She shared with him how both she and her mother became radical believers in Jesus Christ after she was found miraculously alive. Pastor Habib was impressed by Anahid's vibrant testimony in spite of the fact that she had lost both her legs and was struggling to care for her toddler.

With help from NCM and Armenian Nazarene churches in America, Anahid was able to get prostheses in America. Since most individuals who lost limbs could not be assisted in this manner, Pastor Habib recommended to NCM that a sewing factory be opened in Gyumri.

A year later, 25 sewing machines and several heavy irons, knitting machines, electric scissors, and button-makers were airlifted to Armenia with the help of a member of the nation's parliament. The mayor of Gyumri, impressed with NCM's vision to help the community, donated land for the sewing factory. Plans progressed. The three-story building would house a sewing factory, a church, and two apartments. The next year the cement was already poured when the unthinkable happened—the Soviet Union collapsed! Soon electricity was only running a half hour a day. Undaunted, the group purchased a gas generator and sewed in an old warehouse, but soon there was no fuel available for the generator.

In 1996 Maggie Bailey was invited by Point Loma Nazarene University (PLNU) to meet with its business faculty to brainstorm ways in which they might globalize their business program. Dr. Bailey's experience included creating an international business program for the University of Redlands in Cali-

(L. to r.): **Armenian youth, Pastor Karen, Sam Doctorian, Armenian woman, Maggie Bailey, and Pastor Seryan**

fornia and a study abroad program for Cambridge University in England.

Two years later, Dr. Bailey traveled to Armenia with four other interested people to see how PLNU could partner with sustainable efforts in Armenia.

Dr. Bailey describes the visit. "When we drove into Gyumri, we were shocked to find people still living in the shipping containers that brought relief supplies and in dilapidated Soviet high-rises. The entire region had been denuded of trees for firewood to stave off the bitter winters. Many people were without arms and legs from the earthquake. The picture was one of total hopelessness.

"I sat in the back of the bus, shielding my eyes so no one could see my tears. 'O God,' I prayed, 'just get me out of here, and I will never come back. Forgive me for my arrogance in thinking I could do anything to bring economic development.' I looked out over an arid plain without a tree or sign of life. God reminded me then of the valley of dry bones when He asked Ezekiel if the bones could live again (Ezekiel 37). That is when I said, 'Lord, I am available.'"

As a result of this experience, Dr. Bailey joined the faculty at PLNU, and the Armenian Center for International Development was birthed. Dr. Bailey has since led several work teams to Armenia.

Gina Rice, then student body president of PLNU, traveled with Dr. Bailey in 2000. For two weeks they visited the poorest regions of Armenia with the executive director of Armenian Relief and Development Association (ARDA). Gina wrote in her journal: "It's easy to get overwhelmed by the magnitude of the need. I was in homes of refugees, forgotten elderly, and mothers who were starving so their children could eat. When I know the pile of grass heaped on a woman's table is what she plans on feeding her family for the day, I know there is much to be done. Jesus calls us, very clearly, to feed, clothe, visit, and simply love."

The next year a team of 12 from PLNU journeyed to Gyumri for a variety of compassionate ministries. They conducted health assessments on over 400 kindergarten students and 250 elderly people. The students bought food for families living in the shipping containers, served in a soup kitchen, and assisted in four hospitals in Yerevan. The volunteers learned to work with no running water, inadequate toilet facilities, and poor lighting. "It was an incredible challenge to work under such adverse circumstances," Dr. Bailey reflects. "But I don't think we'll ever forget the children receiving their first

A shipping-container home

toothbrushes and parading around the yard with them raised above their heads. We certainly gained a new appreciation for all we have."

Children are an important aspect of the work in Armenia. In 2002 and 2003 missionary Linda Russell led Youth in Mission teams from Ukraine and Russia to hold Vacation Bible School (VBS) programs. For the first VBS in Gyumri they had materials for 60 children. After 150 registered they had to lock the doors! On the final day of VBS more than 300 adults and children came for a program where Pastor Karen Khachatryan preached the gospel. The seeds planted in these outreach efforts led to the sprouting of the Gyumri Church of the Nazarene.

Children in Armenia, especially those living in metal shipping containers, are often chronically sick with respiratory problems because of the severe winters. Basic medicines like aspirin can cost five times as much as in America. Habib Alajaji and missionaries Chuck and Carla Sunberg coordinated NCM's partnership with ARDA to work cooperatively on a pharmacy to provide reasonably priced medicines to the community. In 2004 ARDA built a health center to house the pharmacy, a diagnostic laboratory, dental clinic, optical lab, and counseling center.

To round out this holistic ministry, a Nazarene church and community center were planned. In 2003 Dr. Bailey led a team to a small town near Gyumri. Land and materials were purchased in partnership with NCM. All construction was done by hand since electricity was not available.

Besides construction, the team sorted, bagged, and delivered 1,200 pounds of clothing, school supplies, and medicines. The ladies purchased food for the 60 families attending the Gyumri church and held a party for the children. Dr. Bailey held a Micro Enterprise Business seminar and conducted on-site research of local businesses in Yerevan to determine what microfinance projects were feasible.

"NCM helps poor bring home the bacon," declared the headline. In 2003 NCM held its first "Pig Conference" with Nazarenes from Armenia, Russia, and Ukraine. A Nazarene layman from Iowa State University, Terry Steinhart, led the training session. To raise funds, PLNU sold T-shirts with the slogan, "Changing Lives, One Pig at a Time." Part of the Akhuryan Nazarene Community Center contains a pig barn. The Community Center will also be used for medical, theological, computer, and business enterprise development for the local region.

(L. to r.): **Pastor Karen, Armenian man, and Pastor Ara**

There is an air of excitement for future ministry for the Nazarene Church in Armenia. Guided by Nazarene leader Karen Khachatryan* and pastors Ara Kodjoyan and Seryan Vardanyan, the group of believers is growing. ARDA is partnering with NCM on several relief shipments each year.

"NCM has opened the door for great ministry opportunities in Armenia," Dr. Bailey stresses, "but the economy of this young Christian community is devastatingly poor and families are literally starving. The vision of PLNU's Armenian Center for International Development is to help Christian communi-

---

*Rev. Khachatryan was ordained in 2005, the first Nazarene in Armenia to be ordained.

ties achieve economic stability to both support the mission of the church and feed their families. This new ministry would link Christian businesspeople from the poorest village churches with those in the West who can offer management and technical resources as well as discipling these new Christians in their faith journey. Armenia could become the model for other world areas."

* * *

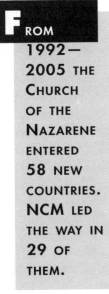

FROM 1992—2005 THE CHURCH OF THE NAZARENE ENTERED 58 NEW COUNTRIES. NCM LED THE WAY IN 29 OF THEM.

A phone ringing in the middle of the night awakened Habib Alajaji. Robert Scott, then World Mission director, was calling from Moscow. He had just been told by a Russian government official, "We know the Nazarenes. You were the first group who responded with practical rehabilitation efforts in Armenia. You delivered what you promised." Because of compassionate ministries in Armenia, the church had received the green light to enter Russia in 1992.

Unconditional assistance. Intentional evangelism. NCM's simple formula is bringing unparalleled opportunities for the holiness message to reach new countries and people groups.

From 1992—2005 the Church of the Nazarene entered 58 new countries. NCM led the way in 29 of them. Here is the list with the dates of official entry.

1992
Bangladesh
Cambodia
Ethiopia
Romania
Russia
Ukraine

1993
Albania
Madagascar

1994
Bulgaria
Creative Access Area 3

1996
Kazakhstan
Pakistan

1998
Nepal

1999
Creative Access Area 1
Creative Access Area 5
Poland
Sudan

2000
Creative Access Area 2
Macedonia
Sri Lanka
Tonga

2001
Creative Access Area 4
East Timor

2002
Armenia
Creative Access Area 6

2003
Creative Access Area 9

2004
Guinea-Bissau

2005
Kosovo

2006
Iraq

4
ONE INFRASTRUCTURE, MANY PARTNERS

Have you ever wondered how Nazarene Compassionate Ministries can be on the spot when disaster strikes almost anywhere on the globe? The answer has many faces. In fact, it has several thousand faces—those of Nazarene missionaries, local pastors, and compassionate laypeople prepared to mobilize the church around the world. They provide a highly effective infrastructure for a quick response in times of crisis.

When a volcanic eruption spewed a mile-wide, six-foot-high wall of burning lava down Mount Nyiragongo in the Democratic Republic of Congo, Nazarene missionaries Jon Kroeze and Russ Frazier were quickly on-site to distribute relief supplies and food to hundreds of Nazarene families who had lost everything.

When 70 Nazarene families fled for their lives into Ethiopia and several were killed, a Nazarene missionary was there to mobilize food, emergency supplies, Bibles, and grief counseling to our distraught brothers and sisters.

When Hurricane Iris destroyed corn crops in Guatemala, missionary Kris Ryan and local Nazarenes helped unload 20 tons of corn. Half was shared among Nazarene churches and half went to widows and orphans in an economically depressed area.

Because people give to the World Evangelism Fund (WEF), there are more than 800 Nazarene missionaries working alongside local leaders and churches. This infrastructure helps NCM tremendously since it does not receive WEF money and relies solely on donations. Relief workers are usually volunteers from local Nazarene churches, so there's no need to set up distribution offices. There is accountability for funds because local leaders know the people who received the aid. When disaster strikes, this infrastructure is a valuable network for compassion.

With the growth of the church has come the challenge of internal resources not being sufficient to meet the vast needs. Bob Remington, a layperson from Canada, realized back in 1980 that partnerships for large projects would be necessary. He worked with missionaries David Falk and Bill Moon on a transformer for Swaziland. With a price tag of $100,000, Remington arranged for Canadian Nazarene offerings to be matched by the government of the province of Alberta, and the transformer became a reality. Steve Weber, the first director of NCM International, built on Remington's dream of taking Nazarene money and multiplying it through partnerships.

Today the Church of the Nazarene is involved in projects of compassion in the hundreds of thousands—even millions of dollars. For example, in

2004 the southern Africa drought was in its third year, and each year the situation became more critical and the needs greater. The Nazarene church had almost 100,000 members in the six countries most affected. Prolonged feeding of Nazarene families was a $2-million project. In situations like this, partnerships from other relief organizations, corporations, and individuals are vital.

SOUTHERN AFRICA FAMINE

Water as far as the eye could see. Nazarenes stranded in trees and on rooftops. This is what Bob Prescott, then NCM director, saw as he flew over Mozambique during the great floods of 2000. Two years later as a little Cessna 206 flew him over five southern Africa countries, he saw brown fields of withered crops and dusty villages. The severe drought conditions caused the World Health Organization to declare it the greatest humanitarian crisis in the world at the time, with more than 60 million people at risk.

Traveling with Bob Prescott were Heinz and Patricia Schubert, then Nazarene Disaster Relief Africa coordinators, and Kelly Miller, disaster director of World Concern. As they witnessed food distributions in Malawi and Mozambique, Mr. Miller was most impressed. "I had no idea the Nazarenes had this kind of presence and distribution system in Africa," Kelly stated. His report prompted World Concern to send NCM $68,000 for famine relief.

With a project this immense, it takes many partners! The Canadian Foodgrains Bank funded 275 tons of corn and rice. The Food Resources Bank gave over $300,000 to plant community gardens for AIDS orphans and caregivers, in hopes rain would come. These funding partners recognize the value of the in-place delivery system that the Nazarenes have in 150 world areas.

As in any project, donations from churches and individuals are vitally important. One donor gave $64,000 to ship nine containers of beans from Canada to Angola, Zambia, and Mozambique. The same donor also gave $180,000 to feed 1,440 families for five months and to give each family 22 pounds of seeds to replant their fields when the rains came.

Another donor contributed several hundred kilos of maize for Lesotho. A group of Nazarene volunteers traveled over isolated mountains into the remote wilderness to deliver the sacks of grain to starving Christians there. When one vehicle caught fire, they feverishly worked in the flames to pull out the grain. Though the vehicle was consumed by fire, the volunteers rescued seven large bags of maize and carried them up the mountain to feed the people.

Other African countries partnered in the relief efforts. Faculty and students of Africa Nazarene University gave to pastors in Malawi. The NYI in Kenya gave maize meal and beans for Zambia.

Around the world, people chipped in to help. Helmer Juárez, NCM coordinator for the MAC Region, encouraged his region to "Take Jesus to Dinner." They sent in $3,300 for famine efforts.

John Wilcox, Nazarene pastor in California, found 222 dimes in a year. When he read in an

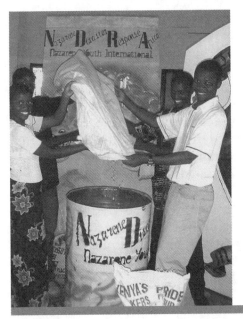

NYI in Kenya providing grain for Zambia

NCM press release "It takes only 10 cents (U.S.) to feed a starving person in Africa," he knew why God had placed dimes in his path. He shared his story, and people began to give.

A little girl sent Rev. Wilcox 100 dimes she had saved along with a note, "Dear Pastor, please feed the hungry babies for me. Love, Liana." Two women who had saved dimes for years for a vacation gave them instead to feed the starving in Africa. Rev. Wilcox's church had a goal of 5,000 dimes; 11,048 came in on the first Sunday! The entire Northern

California District has decided to make this an annual event for Nazarene Compassionate Ministries, calling it "December Dimes," with a goal of 500,000 dimes their first year.

Pastor Caleb Herrera of the Las Palmas Church of the Nazarene in San Antonio wrote: "Your story (the NCM press release) was so moving that our church board has decided to send every dime from every service to compassionate ministries."

Trino Jara, NCM coordinator for the Africa Region, shares, "Sometimes I have worried because we don't have much money for the vast needs of the Africans suffering from so many tragedies. Then the Lord gives me peace as He reminds me that He is in control. He will provide. It is not the church that serves; it is the living God coming to serve His people through us. Thank you so much for your help! It is our hope that thousands of lives in Zambia, Zimbabwe, Malawi, Mozambique, and Lesotho will be impacted by the living gospel of our Lord Jesus Christ."

That hope was realized in all five countries, but especially in Zambia.

ZAMBIA

"We saw firsthand the people who were starving," shares Gary Sidle, whose family arrived in Zambia for missionary service in the midst of the drought. "People were eating roots and grasses. The great news was that NCM had already trained an NCM committee in every local church. These committees helped speed up the work and provided a

Food distribution in Zambia

network for large-scale relief efforts to begin, to be implemented, and to provide follow-up evaluations."

One layperson in particular, Laston Mwale, rallied the people of Chikumbi Church of the Nazarene. Mr. Mwale is a farmer with a good understanding of agriculture. His Christlike compassion for the people living around Chikumbi and his organizational skills were a tremendous asset.

Organized under the excellent leadership of Gary Sidle and Gilbert Bakasa, Zambia NCM coordinator, the relief effort for 3,600 families was so well done that the Zambian government issued public statements encouraging all relief work to follow the example of the Church of the Nazarene. A newspaper in Zambia reported: "Over 2,000 families in

Thyolo District will enjoy this year's Christmas without starving because Nazarene Disaster Response distributed 50-kg (110 lb.) bags of maize flour to each family." A letter from the office of the Zambia's president said, "On behalf of the Republic of Zambia, I wish to thank the Church of the Nazarene for the hospitality and generosity shown to our people at the time of greatest need."

Rev. Bakasa shares his strategy for NCM in Zambia. "The people need food, but they also need God. Food is temporary, but a relationship with God is forever. When the village chiefs welcomed us, we went. We fed people maize and beans, and spiritually we fed them the *JESUS* film. Almost every chief has invited us back to begin a church in his community."

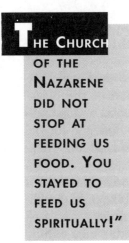

THE CHURCH OF THE NAZARENE DID NOT STOP AT FEEDING US FOOD. YOU STAYED TO FEED US SPIRITUALLY!"

With 26 new churches in Zambia, Rev. Sidle immediately tackled the huge challenge of discipleship and training of the new converts. When he went back to a village to begin discipling, one new Christian greeted him cheerfully. "You could be back to help us bury our families who were starving," the layman told Rev. Sidle, "but instead we are celebrating today what God has done through NCM and the Church of the Nazarene." The man, now a lay pastor in a Nazarene church, is taking theological classes.

Zambia is 85 percent agricultural. Between the

years of drought and the high prevalence of AIDS, poverty and unemployment are stark realities in the congregations. Pastors across Zambia are overwhelmed with visiting the sick and performing funerals. Yet six months after the food distribution ended, a couple of dozen churches had been started. With the blessings of tremendous spiritual growth have come great challenges—48 new churches need pastors. Praise God, there are 42 enrolled at two new extension education centers.

The revival that began in drought is bringing showers of blessings. More new churches are anticipated as the Holy Spirit sweeps across the country. One man said, "This message of holiness is what we have needed to hear!" Another said, "I am so pleased the Church of the Nazarene did not stop at feeding us food. You stayed to feed us spiritually!" These success stories in Zambia would not have been possible without the Nazarene infrastructure and many partners like World Concern, Food Resources Bank, Canadian Foodgrains Bank, Nazarene churches, and individuals. Oh yes, and all those dimes!

❊　❊　❊

Partnerships. NCM depends on them. When the wheels on the buses at the Nazarene schools in Jordan refused to "go round and round," the situation became so critical the schools were in jeopardy of closing. These schools have been effectively serving Middle East families for over 50 years.

Help for Brethren, a partner organization in Germany, agreed to raise $46,000 for one bus if

New school bus for Jordan

NCM could match that amount for the other bus. That's a lot of money! Gerald Oliver Sr. put the need before the Eastern Mediterranean Partnership, and John Seaman challenged people to buy bus seats for $500 each. Between the partnership group and individuals who responded to an appeal in *NCM Today*, the entire $46,000 came in.

Partnering with NCM allows ordinary individuals to accomplish extraordinary things together for God's kingdom.

ONE X ONE = TEN

Wouldn't you love to have Jesus as your math teacher? It would be so much fun. After all, you'd never know quite what to expect from Him when it came to multiplication.

Remember the story in John 6 where a young boy gives his five loaves and two fish to Jesus? The Lord took that small offering, added His blessing, and multiplied it beyond anyone's expectations. He's still doing the same today.

"THE FISH"

It was a gaudy blanket from the 1960s era. It even had a rip in it. But one of the volunteers at the Compassionate Resource Warehouse (CRW) in Victoria, British Columbia, saw potential in it. She lovingly repaired it and shipped it off to Africa.

A woman with AIDS in Kenya had prayed for a bright and colorful blanket. When she received this blanket, she thanked the Lord for loving her this much. "I can die in peace now," she told the person who handed her the blanket, "because I have a blanket to be buried in." Two days later she passed away and was tenderly buried in her blanket from God.

"The Lord used that blanket to minister to His

child during her dying days, to reinforce His love for her," reflects Dell Marie Wergeland, director of CRW. "It also allowed her to fulfill the custom of her community and die with dignity, not in a pauper's grave. It's stories like this that give me the passion to do what I'm doing."

Dell is a spunky, petite dynamo that volunteers 40/60-hour weeks, leading a task force of 86 volunteers, ages 10 to 94. Her passion began with relief work in 1999 following Hurricane Mitch in Honduras. Upon her return home, Dell worked with a group of friends to gather clothes, school supplies, household items, medical supplies, and funds to ship a container of goods to the destitute in Honduras. It took them a year.

During those 12 months, Dell began to feel her heart drawn to this ministry. A nurse by profession, Dell knew there were impoverished people around the globe who desperately needed supplies. Scripture that inspired her was 2 Corinthians 9:11-12. "Basically these verses say that God will give you a lot so you can give away a lot," says Dell. "When we take our gifts to those who need them, they will break out in praise to God. So two good things happen when you give: those in need are helped, and they overflow with thanks to God."

When Dell began, everything seemed stacked against this new ministry. Although E.Y. Construction donated warehouse space for three years, it is located on an island where there are scarce resources, the economy is slow, and supplies had to be shipped on ferries, increasing the costs. "It should not

Dell Marie Wergeland

have worked here," says Dell, "but try telling God that!"

Though it began with one shipment in 2000, in the next two years CRW shipped 60 huge containers. When the three years of donated space ended, it took less than six weeks to raise the funds to buy the warehouse—with a price tag of $300,000.

At the end of 2002, shipments valued at $13.3 million had cost only a little over $12,000 to send. A few months later the Nazarene church received containers worth $1.6 million, for which NCM Canada paid $13,000. Do the math—that's paying less than 1 percent of the full value. Total volunteer hours that year came to a whopping 19,701, or almost 493 40-hour workweeks!

CRW volunteers are the key. They pack boxes and check to assure contents are clean and in good repair. One group washes and mends clothing and bedsheets. Another group hand-knits teddy bears; more than 20,000 of them have been sent. Other volunteers make things like sweaters or toys. Still others help with the heavy labor of lifting and packing the trucks. There is even a volunteer webmaster for CRW. "God is opening doors in many countries previously closed to the Gospel," one volunteer says. "What an incredible thing He is doing—and He uses little ol' me!"

"One time we sent a container of beds to a hospital in the Philippines," Dell shares. "It was incredibly moving to hear how they literally lifted people up off the ground and placed them on beds. For this small hospital of hydrocephalic patients, it was the first time they were able to partially sit up and view the world."

Another time CRW sent a shipment to an area that decided to give men's ties to their pastors at district assembly. One pastor had been so discouraged he was ready to quit. When he heard he would receive a tie, he asked the Lord, "If you love me and want me to continue as a pastor, please give me a sign. Please give me an orange tie." At the district assembly the district superintendent opened up the box of ties and went down the line giving each pastor a tie. When he came to this pastor, he pulled out an orange tie. The superintendent started to put it back because of the odd color, but the pastor began weeping and said, "This is the tie for me."

IT MAY SURPRISE YOU TO KNOW THAT THERE IS PLENTY OF FOOD IN THE WORLD FOR EVERYONE.

"What are the odds of someone donating an orange tie," Dell comments, "and it being delivered to that exact country, to that exact district assembly, to that exact pastor? Our amazing God is working through us to meet needs that otherwise wouldn't be met. Through us He is sending the message that someone in the world cares. He is multiplying our efforts in remarkable ways, all because we daily give to Him our small 'fish'!"

"THE BREAD"

"A young mother in the Domasi township of Malawi stood wearily in the long line, waiting since before dawn to buy a few grains of scarce corn," reported NCM in 2002. "The sun was beginning to set when she began to wail and could not be consoled. Her 10-month-old baby on her back could wait no longer. He had died from hunger."

It may surprise you to know that there is plenty of food in the world for everyone. Enough food is produced to provide at least 4.3 pounds of food per person per day: 2.5 pounds of grain, beans, and nuts; about one pound of fruits and vegetables; and nearly another pound of meat, milk, and eggs—enough to make most people fat! The problem is that many of the world's people do not have access to the resources to produce or purchase food. That's where Canadian Foodgrains Bank (CFGB) comes in.

Elaine Bumstead *(left)* with Elizabeth Musimbi, NCM coordinator for East Africa

CFGB is comprised of 13 different Christian church and relief organizations, of which the Church of the Nazarene is one. It was formed as a Christian response to hunger in 1983. Each of the 13 members raises money and grain donations in their churches and throughout rural Canada. Approximately 40 percent is grain and 60 percent cash. These are then "deposited" into the CFGB for use in times of disaster.

The Church of the Nazarene is well-represented at CFGB through NCM Canada and Elaine Bumstead, who became a member of its board of directors in 2000. Elaine first became interested in the work of CFGB in the mid-1990s when she was a local missions president at Kolapore Church of the Nazarene.

"Many of the farmers in surrounding towns would not attend church," Elaine says, "but would attend a harvest celebration since they are passionate about farming. So each year we had a potluck dinner on a flatbed wagon in a field and shared with community farmers how they can make a global difference by donating some of their crops."

At CFGB Elaine's primary responsibility is to program food on behalf of NCM Canada. She also travels to countries to train Nazarene national leaders in fulfilling CFGB's application requirements. In Canada she resources churches with educational curriculum and encourages donations, using the slogan "Food for All."

Elaine was called to this ministry while in Bangladesh, a poor country that experiences frequent flooding and food shortages. "I was walking through the villages and feeling overwhelmed by such tremendous needs," recalls Elaine, "when the Lord spoke to me and reminded me that I could contribute to the solution of those needs." From that moment on, Elaine has not regretted giving God her "loaves" for His use.

God has multiplied Elaine's efforts on behalf of the Church of the Nazarene, as she has built on the excellent foundation begun at CFGB by David Falk, Glenn Follis, and John Watton. The CFGB has built up such an international reputation that recently the Canadian government agreed to match most of their donations on a 4:1 ratio, up to $16 million per year.

In 2003 the Church of the Nazarene was involved with CFGB in 12 projects, most of which were funded at the 4:1 ratio.

Ready for some more math? One Canadian Nazarene donates $1, either cash or grain value, to CFGB. That $1 is multiplied by CFGB who then partners with the Canadian government for more multiplication. Therefore, one person donating $1 yields $10 (1 x 1 = 10)!

"It's like a grain-carrying train in Canada 10 miles long," explains Elaine. "The first mile of the train is donated by Canadian Nazarenes and the last 9 miles are donated by CFGB and the Canadian government. As we have tried to reach out to hungry people around the world, God has truly multiplied our loaves of bread!"

> COMPASSION AS A LIFESTYLE *IS* ABOUT COUNTING OUR BLESSINGS AND TALLYING UP OUR GRATEFULNESS.

GOD'S MATH

Compassion as a lifestyle is not about calculating the cost. It's not about dividing the Kingdom between them and us. It's not about adding up our good deeds or tracking the numbers.

Compassion as a lifestyle *is* about counting our blessings and tallying up our gratefulness. It's about asking God to help us be an answer to the world's problems. It's about trusting Him to take our loaves and fishes and multiply them beyond our expectations.

"Now to him who is able to do immeasurably more than all we ask or imagine, according to his power that is at work within us" (Ephesians 3:20).

✳ ✳ ✳

Want to offer up *your* loaves and fishes? Go to the Web site for creative ideas on collecting clothes and Crisis Care Kits. (See the Compassionate Ministry Resources, page 91.)

ONE CHILD AT A TIME

Touching the life of a child is one of life's most fulfilling callings. Helping a child receive training, education, or food can break generational cycles of poverty, keep a child alive, or make it possible for the parents to serve in ministry. Nazarene Compassionate Ministries has provided opportunities for sponsors to have a powerful influence in the lives of children since 1985. Only heaven will reveal the thousands of lives impacted by caring sponsors.

FROM A TRAGIC PAST TO A HOPE-FILLED FUTURE

Their grandfather died following the advice of a witch doctor. Their aunt was killed by her husband in a fit of rage. Khulisile (Khuli) and Khumbuzile (Khumbu) Dlamini were born into a tribe that considered twins a curse, and at one time killed the second twin born. Their mother died giving them birth, and their father, who already had 14 children, would not claim them. These tiny twins, born into tragedy and darkness in rural Swaziland, should not have survived. But God had plans for a future filled with hope for Khuli and Khumbu.

Gladys Mantombi Dlamini, a Nazarene pastor

in Swaziland, went to grieve with the family after the mother's death. Dismayed at the spiritual darkness she found, she sensed God calling her to raise Khuli and Khumbu. She brought them home at two weeks old, so tiny she was afraid they wouldn't survive the ride over the bumpy road.

Gladys describes becoming a single mother. "The first night they had diarrhea, and I realized I had no spare cloth diapers. *What am I doing?* I suddenly thought. *I have no clothes for them. I'm single. I live in a tiny one-bedroom cement-block house. What can I give them?* But deep in my heart I rejoiced as I looked at those two tiny babies. I so desperately wanted to give them a chance to be raised in a Christian home and receive an education. I stood there and prayed for God to provide a way. I asked Him to bless my efforts to save their souls from witch doctors and practices not pleasing to Him."

God answered that prayer through NCM's Child Sponsorship (CS) program. Khumbu and Khuli were among the first to be enrolled when the program began in 1985. From then until 1996 when they graduated from high school, they never failed a class. Gladys attributes it to prayer, the quality of the CS program, and the kindness of Nazarene missionaries.

"We had some rough times," Gladys recalls. "One day when they were in first grade, they were taunted for not having a 'real' mother and a father. Doris Gailey, one of the missionaries, found me crying behind the faculty office at the Bible college. She gave me gentle advice and prayed with me. And I'm so appreciative of two other missionaries, Dana

Khulisile

Khumbuzile

Harding and Kathryn Savage, who treated Khumbu and Khuli like daughters."

"Auntie" Dana and "Auntie" Kathy have been there for Khuli and Khumbu since Gladys brought them home. They helped with medical bills, eyeglasses, and school trips. Thanks to Dana and Kathy, the girls were given an opportunity to attend Olivet Nazarene University (ONU). Khuli remembers their first night at Olivet, "We just couldn't believe we were in America. We stayed up all night staring at each other."

CHILD SPONSORSHIP TRULY GAVE US "A HOPE AND A FUTURE."

In 2002 *Kids Today* ran a story on the twins. After it was published it was discovered that the son of the Meo family, Khuli's sponsors from grades 1 through 12, also attended ONU. Professor Mark Bishop had the privilege of introducing Khuli to Joshua Meo. Khuli was able to thank Joshua and his family for the role they played in her life.

"I remember growing up and seeing these pictures of a little girl on our fridge," Joshua says. "It's really cool how the Lord worked it out for me to meet Khuli. Obviously there's a miracle in this, to have the privilege to see firsthand how our family's sponsorship made a difference. Because I've met Khuli, I can tell people child sponsorship really works!"

Khuli and Khumbu share what it was like to be sponsored. "It was fun to receive notes and pictures from our sponsors. They always made us feel special. As little girls growing up in Swaziland, God gave us a vision of getting a good education in America, and then we would be prepared to help the poverty of our people in Africa. Child Sponsorship truly gave us 'a hope and a future' (Jeremiah 29:11). We want to serve Christ all our lives because we've been given so much."

Khumbu graduated in 2002 with a B.A. in family consumer science and minors in social work and psychology. She is working toward a master's degree in psychology and professional counseling. Khuli graduated in 2003 with a bachelor's in business administration and management, and the following year she married Kudakwashe Mudavanhu from Zimbabwe.

Both of the twins enjoy singing and have performed with the South African Cultural Arts Organization. Their goal is to return to Africa and help with the AIDS crisis.

What does their mother, Gladys, think of her twins now? "They are God's children, nurtured by His church through child sponsorship, and now they are ready to answer His call to service."

ORPHANED, BUT NOT ABANDONED

Hernesto and Hermelinda Toj were in the first group of 45 children who were left at the Hogar del Niño (Home of the Child) in San Miguel Chicaj, Guatemala, when it first opened in 1985. Today they are in their early 30s.

They both finished elementary school with their

sponsors' support. Hernesto went on and finished secondary school with a concentration in accounting. Thanks in large part to a $36,000 donation to the orphanage for carpentry training from NCM Canada, Hernesto learned the trade of carpentry. Hermelinda studied sewing and dressmaking for her vocational training. She received a manual sewing machine, paid for from the monthly support of her sponsor.

As young adults, Hernesto and Hermelinda fell in love and married. Today they live near San Gabriel about five miles from the Home of the Child and have four children of their own. Hernesto is an accountant and a carpenter; Hermelinda tends a

A Guatemalan girl in the Child Sponsorship ministry

small store in their home. Hernesto has been recognized for his leadership in the community. At the time this book was written, he was a candidate for mayor of the municipality of San Miguel. Dedicated laypeople, they attend the San Gabriel Nazarene Church with their children.

Child sponsorship gave Hernesto and Hermelinda the opportunity for education, vocations, meeting, and marrying. Now they are returning that investment through responsible leadership in the church and community. Praise God for Nazarene Child Sponsorship.

"Sew" Very Thankful

Alberta was from the Maya town of Rabinal. Both of her parents were killed in the civil conflict that plagued Guatemala for almost 30 years. When she arrived at the Hogar del Niño in 1985, she was a very scared nine-year-old.

Alberta finished primary school. She received a manual sewing machine and studied sewing and dressmaking at the Home. At age 18 she went to Guatemala City to look for work. Because she knew how to sew, she was able to get a job working in a large clothing factory.

Alberta, skilled and diligent, worked hard. Before long the factory owners selected her for a two-year, all-expense-paid training program in Korea to prepare her for company management. She completed the training and returned to Guatemala where she worked several years for the company.

Alberta met a young man from her hometown

who had also come to Guatemala City. They married and moved back to Rabinal to raise a family. There they are active in the local Nazarene church. Alberta is so thankful that the CS program gave her an opportunity for education, training, work, and now a happy family back home. God's love and child sponsorship gave her a future and a hope.

WON BY ONE

One-on-one evangelism is a powerful way to reach people for Christ, especially in predominantly Muslim communities. Friendship and trust are vital, as you will see in this story of Kosovo* and the new believers who were won by one.

✳ ✳ ✳

Destruction was everywhere. Isuf and his son Ylber ran to the mountains. There they hid and watched the bombing of their village. Two days later they ventured back down the mountain. For two months they did not know which family members were alive or dead. When they saw their home gutted, Isuf cried out, "Oh, God, help me. I have only burnt walls and no roof. Please send someone to save us from this cold winter."

God was already working on the answer. At the time of Isuf's heartbroken cry, Nazarene congregations in Albania were ministering to some of the 900,000 refugees who had fled Kosovo during the war in early 1999. Missionaries David and Sandra Allison, with the help of Nazarene Compassionate

---

*Kosovo is called Kosova by the locals.

Rebuilding a roof in Kosovo

Ministries, distributed food, clothing, diapers, hygiene items, bedding, and dishes to over 300 households who had taken in 6 to 50 refugees each. The refugees, almost entirely Muslim, also received invitations to Nazarene services. Many visited, and one was saved, 15-year-old Imir Gashi.

During the conflict approximately 78,000 houses had been torched. Bob Prescott, NCM director at the time, felt led to help rebuild roofs in this country that had no Nazarene work. In 1999 an assessment team traveled to Kosovo. One late afternoon, on impulse, they stopped at a village where every house looked burned. The villagers told NCM they were the first outsiders to come to Shirok. Team members sensed this was the place that needed them the most.

With less than two weeks notice, a gifted team of eight volunteers arrived in Kosovo for a two-month stay. Bob and Carol Fogle, Josh Loring, Clayton Prescott, Ron and Sue Allen, and Josh Allen accompanied team leader Dan Dillon. The team decided to stay a third month, with the exception of Ron and Sue Allen, who were replaced by Doug and Twila Ward. The team's expertise consisted of two ministers, two children's workers, two youth workers, two carpenters, three musicians, two cooks, one nurse, and one interpreter.

A country that has recently experienced war can be challenging. The team was often without electricity, sometimes for as long as five days. When they had no water, baths were taken from a Crock-Pot and a cup. They created a coffeemaker from a two-liter soda bottle and mashed their potatoes with the bottom of a mayo jar. Bedroom temperatures sometimes reached 28 degrees Fahrenheit; frequently they slid into frigid sheets at night and awoke to frozen water in the sink. Yet the work advanced in a great spirit of camaraderie, including one fun night by candlelight when they made up song lyrics in the we-have-no-electricity blues genre.

Out of 202 homes in Shirok, 120 were severely damaged. With the help of the local commissioner, the families most in need were chosen for the team to build roofs and weatherize one room in each. Weatherization involved providing a window and door, wiring the room for electricity, plastering the walls, installing a wood-burning stove, and paneling the ceiling.

Remember Imir, the young man who was saved in Albania? He "just happened" to live three miles from Shirok. The team helped haul five wagonloads of debris from Imir's home, and two neighbors accepted the Lord that day. (More of Imir's incredible story is in chapter 8.)

(L. to r.): **Bob Fogle, Imir, and Josh Allen**

As the team worked on the top floors, they were exposed to the sky and sometimes snow as they shoveled rubbish and water. They hoisted up timbers to replace the burned ones. Isuf, the man who cried out to God for help, was amazed to receive a new roof.

During the breaks, Twila Ward and Carol Fogle would sometimes take prayer walks around the neighborhood. The people of Kosovo are incredibly hospitable, and often they invited Twila and Carol in for *caj* (tea).

"As we sat and sipped tea," Carol says, "we were surrounded by windows blown out, walls charred black, ceilings with holes, wires hanging from walls, glass and burnt splinters everywhere. As people cleaned up their homes, they would sing in their language 'Kosova, we love you, we are coming home.' Their resilience is incredible. Kosova quickly became not just a place in Europe but a place in our hearts."

During one of the visits they learned the 32-year-old husband had been killed, leaving behind his wife and four children under 10 years. When the team gave the children crayons, the 9-year-old drew a picture of a house with flames shooting from it, tanks shooting at it, and a helicopter overhead. The open, raw grief of this family needed no translation. The team's presence was a statement of love for the people of Kosovo. They were often asked why they came to Shirok, giving them opportunities to share how Christ's love compelled them to come.

The team introduced a new custom to the village—potluck dinners. They invited everyone to a meal and a showing of the *JESUS* film. About 200 people came. All the children received donated softballs, and Don Moore, missionary from Macedonia, organized a softball-throwing contest. The film was the first time that many heard the entire story of Christ. As a team member was walking home with a flashlight late at night, a young man approached him and said, "I saw your light and wondered if you wanted to share it." This young Muslim man began to attend the Bible studies and soon met the Light of the world.

More volunteers arrived in Kosovo in 2000, and even more during the next two years. They conducted Bible studies several nights a week in different homes.

Women gathered for crafts, tea, and Bible study. Teen girls enjoyed sewing and English lessons along with Bible study. Computer classes were offered on five computers donated by Food for the Hungry. More roofs were built. Volunteer Ramona Graham even led aerobics classes (behind closed doors!) for the women.

Kid's Club, a program for children, soon had over 100 in attendance. The boys and girls enjoyed the novelty of balloons, Cat's Cradle yarn games, and hearing the Christmas story for the first time. Then suddenly for a week not a single child came to the center. The reason? The local school director had threatened school expulsion for children who attended Kid's Club. NCM sent out a press release asking for prayer. Eventually the director relented and even requested a copy of the *JESUS* film for the school library.

* * *

God has been transforming lives in Kosovo.

Astrit saw the *JESUS* film from his balcony the night of the potluck dinner. It was the first time he had heard of Jesus. He asked many questions for over two years. On February 14, 2002, he gave Jesus the valentine gift of his heart.

The Gashi family lost 23 family members in the war. As the NCM team had devotions every day while building their roof, the 19-year old son, Arjan, listened carefully. One day he announced, "There is something I believe now, but I must say it with my mouth. I believe that God loves me, and I can be

75

saved and assured of heaven if I am born again." The angels rejoiced that day as Arjan prayed to receive Christ.

Team members gave New Testaments with salvation scriptures highlighted to any who expressed an interest. Selim was one. Several weeks later when Josh Allen presented the gospel to him, he replied, "I have been reading this book. I now believe with all my heart."

Elmi was raised in a Muslim family. He was saved in the NCM Bible study. Two days later he was with Clayton Prescott when the local mosque began calling people to prayer. Elmi had an odd look on his face, so Clayton asked him if he was thinking of going. "No!" Elmi replied emphatically. "I'm a new person because I gave my heart to Jesus."

A young man named Ilir also became a Christian, and several months later he led his friend Shkelzim to the Lord.

"I went to Kosovo to tell people about Jesus," Clayton says. "But it is even better when the people I've told begin to tell others!" Won by one, the gospel took root in Kosovo.

In May 2003 Glenn and Jill Noble and their two daughters, Jenna and Alyssa, arrived in Kosovo for two years. These Nazarene volunteers faced challenges too. Five years after the conflict ended, Kosovo still had rolling blackouts every six hours. "We have thrown out the window all known rules about germs," Jill writes, "since at people's houses we eat from a communal dish in the center of the table. There are many stores here, and all sell exactly the

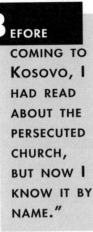

BEFORE COMING TO KOSOVO, I HAD READ ABOUT THE PERSECUTED CHURCH, BUT NOW I KNOW IT BY NAME."

same few things. Sometimes there are 22 people sleeping at our house."

"Many of the meals here are based on yogurt, or kos," Glenn adds. "My relationship with yogurt is pretty much love/hate. People love to serve it to me and . . . !"

The Nobles soon realized Kosovo is not an easy place to be a believer. "The new Christians here face persecution daily," Glenn says. "They have been beaten by their parents, ridiculed by friends, shunned by their families, threatened with expulsion from school, and have received death threats. Sometimes I have to meet with new believers in secret. Before coming to Kosovo, I had read about the persecuted church, but now I know it by name."

When Glenn and Jill arrived, they found a small core of committed believers. Due to persecution, only four or five were gathering together each week. Person by person, the group was once again rebuilt by focusing on relationship building.

Within six months, 25 more people accepted Christ. All are former Muslims. Even though believers understand that baptism is not a means of salvation, they still view it as the point of no return. Four Christians were baptized at a Nazarene camp in Albania in August that year.

Several small groups and a corporate worship service meet weekly. Eighty people are taking En-

The Noble family *(l. to r.)*: Glenn, Jenna, Alyssa, and Jill

glish classes, and all new Christians are being discipled one-on-one. These new believers have even begun their own compassionate ministry of food and clothing to the poor in the surrounding villages.

Perhaps the entire "won by one" success story in Kosovo is best summed up by Fisnik, a young new believer: "I'm thankful for all of you who came with compassion to help. You left the comfort of your homes and the love of your families. Through all of you I have come to realize there is a God and who He is."

Kosovo officially became the 149th world area for the Church of the Nazarene in 2005.

✳ ✳ ✳

There are 865 million unreached Muslims in 3,330 cultural subgroupings.* Most of them will need to be won by one. As the Church of the Nazarene seeks creative ways to enter countries in the challenging 10/40 window, there is a great need for individuals who believe in the power of one to alleviate suffering and reach others with the gospel.

---

*<http://home.snu.edu/~hculbert.fs/1040.htm#facts>

ONE BY ONE

Reaching out to hurting humanity is the very nature of God. When we choose to live incarnately as Christ, His kingdom is ushered in as lives are transformed, one by one.

ONE FAMILY

The newlyweds traveled to 15 African countries as well as India, Nepal, Burma, Thailand, and Hong Kong in nine months. They saw the needs of the world firsthand. John and Laurie Watton say about their travels, "Those experiences really forced us to grapple with the scriptures that direct believers to be involved with the poor and oppressed. We read *Rich Christians in an Age of Hunger* as we traveled through India. Now that was a convicting call!"

As the Wattons returned to Canada, they knew their lives had been forever changed. They became involved in NCM Canada, helping Canadians connect with people around the world who are in desperate need of both compassion and evangelism. John's degree in agriculture served him well as NCM Canada's representative on the board of the Canadian Foodgrains Bank (CFGB).

In 2001 as John was attending a CFGB board meeting, he read a disturbing newspaper article about some religious clashes and ensuing grief in a

West African country. Later in his devotions he restated his willingness to serve, praying: "God, it is our desire to serve You anywhere, but please, Lord, not in this particular West African country!" That country was Nigeria—the very country to which the Church of the Nazarene assigned them as missionaries in 2003.

Both John and Laurie, who felt called to missions as young Christians, say it was their involvement in compassionate ministries that helped nurture that calling. As the NCM coordinator for the West Africa Field, John helps local and national NCM leaders prepare proposals, implement projects, and develop relief capacity to respond to disasters.

"NCM Canada is never far away," says John.

The Watton family *(l. to r.)* **Mitchell, Laurie, John, and Alanna.**

"Containers from Canadian warehouses come to this continent loaded with food, clothes, medical supplies, and Crisis Care Kits. It is an incredible joy to have the privilege to have seen this ministry from both sides—in Canada, to see lives changed as they sort and pack and learn what it is to obey our Lord's command to give to those in need; in Africa, to see lives changed as they realize there is a God who loves them because He called His people to help."

John also serves as the mission coordinator in Nigeria. This involves mission accounting, encouraging district leaders and pastors in their ministries, and overseeing the operation of three theological extension colleges. Laurie Watton, who has a nursing degree, presents seminars on community-health evangelism. She also homeschools their two children, Alanna and Mitchell, who are involved in compassionate outreach as well. Two small business ventures, chicken- and fish-rearing, are being tested by Alanna and Mitchell as possible pension ideas for retiring pastors in West Africa.

"Compassion has an amazing impact," states John. "Compassion changes lives. It has changed ours forever."

ONE COMMUNITY

Prolonged civil conflict in Guatemala had forced hundreds to move wearily from place to place. Finally, they created their home in El Aposento Alto (the Upper Room) in the remote north. Unfortunately, forest fires had killed the palm trees, so there were no branches for roofing material. Their rustic one-room sheds, roofed with plastic sheeting, tore easily.

Two of the families had attended the Nazarene church before they were displaced. They located the North District superintendent, who lived 100 miles away, and asked him to visit their village. The superintendent saw the inadequate living conditions and asked if NCM could provide funds for metal roofing sheets. Each of the 110 houses would need 12 sheets, plus nails and wire, for a total cost of $10,000. NCM could only provide $4,000.

In God's timing, Darin Godby, pastor of the Flemingsburg, Kentucky, Church of the Nazarene, wrote to NCM. He mentioned they were entering a building program, but before they spent money on themselves, they wanted to do something for others. Since their church sponsored a child in Guatemala, were there any possible projects in Guatemala? The Flemingsburg church provided the entire $6,000 remaining for the roofing project.

By helping the community's living conditions, compassion opened the doors to show the *JESUS* film in the village. Forty people accepted Christ. The village showed its appreciation by donating land for a church and providing the labor. The men of the village built the church, and NCM provided cement for the floor. The growing congregation called a pastor, and the church is flourishing.

Compassionate lives, reaching out to hurting humanity, ushered in God's kingdom in this community. *El Aposento Alto* is indeed an "Upper Room" where Christ is Lord.

ONE CHURCH

"Houses were torn off their foundations. Piles of debris littered the streets. We saw endless lines of commercial dump trucks hauling away broken trees and buildings, and we knew that they represented many broken hearts." This account by Rip Wright, pastor of Fawn Grove Church of the Nazarene in Maryland, describes the condition of the flooding in Pineville, West Virginia, in 2000.

Pastor Rip and his wife, Ruth, drove 18 hours round-trip to deliver more than 100 boxes of clothes and Crisis Care Kits. Enthusiastic volunteers from the Pineville Church of the Nazarene were thrilled to receive the items, which were used to meet the urgent needs of community members.

THE WRIGHTS BECAME SUPPORTERS AND CHEERLEADERS OF THE BANANA-BOX MINISTRY.

The Wrights are no strangers to compassionate ministries. When they arrived at Fawn Grove church in 2000, they learned some people had left the church because banana boxes lined the hallways, classrooms, and fellowship hall. Rather than insist they be removed, the Wrights became supporters and cheerleaders of the banana-box ministry.

"A lot of times pastors are told that to win people you have to make your church attractive to them," says Pastor Rip. "But when we read the Bible, we see Jesus doing a lot more washing of dirty feet than trying to make himself look good. What's excit-

John Borgal in the banana-box ministry warehouse

ing is that new people who come are catching the enthusiasm of the congregation to make a difference in our world."

Fawn Grove's interest in compassionate ministries began in the early 1990s through member John Borgal. His contagious passion for compassionate ministries led to thousands of banana boxes passing through their church and shipped around the world. In 2001 the church took a leap of faith and built a 45' x 105' warehouse on church property, which John now oversees full-time. The church board gave NCM, Inc., a 10-year permit to use the building as its shipping center on the east coast of the United States. Attendance at Fawn Grove almost tripled in four years as its compassionate ministries grew.

Ruth and Rip Wright

"Our community knows us as the church that cares," says Ruth Wright. "They know we deliver help and hope to places from Angola to New York City (after 9/11) to Ukraine. Compassionate ministry is a vital part of the Great Commission."

ONE BY ONE

Imir Gashi became a Christian because of compassionate ministries. His spiritual journey began as a refugee in Albania as he responded to the love of Christ shown through NCM there (see chapter 7). After his conversion, Imir immediately became involved in ministry as he helped missionary David Allison with the daily distribution of relief supplies.

After Imir's family moved back to Kosovo, the NCM volunteers who came to rebuild roofs discipled Imir. It wasn't long before Imir felt called into ministry. By the end of the year he had preached his first sermon to some friends. Soon he was assisting in a weekly Bible study, often leading the lessons. One night as he shared about Christ's return, three men accepted Christ. One of them was Selim.

"I want to tell you how I heard the name Jesus Christ for the first time in my life," Selim testifies. "Here in Kosova some American people [from the United States] came in my village to build houses after the war. They visited my family. I couldn't understand all their words because I didn't know good English then. Something new was they prayed before they ate dinner.

"One month later they invited me to a Bible study. I didn't have any idea what this was. They

Selim

gave me a book, and on the first page was a new word I didn't know before: *Bible*. I opened it and read, 'In the beginning God created the heavens and the earth.' From that time I began to feel something in my heart. I kept going to the Bible study, and I listened carefully. In Kosova people who believe in Jesus are in for a dangerous time. But after about a year, I decided I want to be in the family of Jesus. My heart is clear. I have hope and am filled with God's love.

"Now every month we have new believers in Jesus Christ. I am reading the life of Paul. I would like to be like him. I am ready to do everything good in the name of God. The Bible says, 'The LORD is with me; I will not be afraid. What can man do to me?'* God has a big plan for my country. It is happening because you had compassion. God bless you!"

Today both Imir and Selim boldly share their faith. Respected by their peers, both are attending university and working together to plant a church in Prishtina, Kosovo. They are continuing the legacy of compassion evangelism that was modeled for them by NCM volunteers.

And so it continues, God transforming the world through the power of one by one by one.

---

*(Psalm 118:6)

EPILOGUE

Scientists studied a single grass plant, winter rye. For four months they let it grow in a greenhouse, then they removed one cubic inch of soil and counted and measured all the roots. In that short period of time, the winter rye had put forth 378 miles of growth in 14 million distinct roots. That's about three miles a day! As incredible as this is, when experimenters explored further, they discovered that the rye plant had developed 14 billion root hairs. In just one cubic inch of soil, the length of the root hairs totaled 6,000 *miles*.

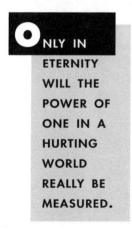

ONLY IN ETERNITY WILL THE POWER OF ONE IN A HURTING WORLD REALLY BE MEASURED.

Compassion as a lifestyle has a similar impact on our world. Too often we say, "I'm just one (cubic inch of soil). What difference can I make?" Yet as we grow in Christlikeness, our compassion puts down roots of His love in others. The most likely way a bitter neighbor will come to know Christ is if someone shows genuine compassion for him. The most likely way we will ever enter the countries in the 10/40 window is through compassionate ministries. The most likely way our churches and homes will experience revival is if some of us start imagining what it is like to live in someone else's skin. Only in eternity will the power of one in a hurting world really be measured.

Edward Everett Hale said, "I am only one, but I am one. I cannot do everything, but I can do something. And because I cannot do everything, I will not refuse to do the something that I can do."

Don't refuse to do the something that you can do. Amazing things can happen when we live like Jesus, compassion as a lifestyle. God has placed each one of us where we are so that we can make a difference—by the power of One!

COMPASSIONATE MINISTRY RESOURCES

NCM
6401 The Paseo
Kansas City, MO 64131
Toll-free: 1-877-NCM-4145
E-mail: <ncm@nazarene.org>
Web site: <www.ncm.org>

NCM/NCMI Relief Shipment Warehouse
Attn.: John Borgal
P.O. Box 117
Fawn Grove, PA 17321-0117
E-mail: <jborgal@ncmi.org>
Phone: 410-452-8699

Compassionate Response Warehouse
Victoria, British Columbia, Canada
E-mail: <werge@telus.net>
Phone: 250-381-GIVE or 250-381-4483
Web site: <www.crwarehouse.ca>

Armenian Center for International Development
School of Business
Point Loma Nazarene University
Phone: 619-849-2305

For information on donating used clothing or
School Pal-Paks, see the NCM, Inc. Web site:
<www.ncmi.org>.

CALL TO ACTION

After reading or listening to *The Power of One*, would you consider doing one or more of the following ideas:

1. Sponsor a child through the NCM Child Sponsorship program. NCM provides the following ideas for child sponsorships:

   - **Children's Class:** Each child receives a drink container or an M&M tube. After emptying, a photo of the sponsored child is glued onto the container. A hole is slit in the top. Children are encouraged to fill the containers with change earned from household chores and bring the money to church.

   - **Adult Class or Small Group:** Have a Child Sponsorship "We CAN Make a Difference" Sunday. On this Sunday, share with your group your desire to sponsor a child. If just 10 people are willing to give 50 cents every Sunday, your group CAN sponsor a child!

   - **Newborn Dedications:** Donate $25 to Child Sponsorship for every newborn dedicated in your church. Present the parents with a certificate that a gift has been given to NCM in honor of their child.

2. Pack a School Pal-Pak or Crisis Care Kit.

3. Stay informed by signing up for free E-mail press releases from NCM.

4. Donate used clothing to one of the NCM warehouses.

5. Donate to NCM through workplace giving via United Way or Combined Federal Campaign.

6. Take a compassionate ministries class through the Continuing Lay Training program. The web site address is <www.clt.nazarene.org>.

7. As a local congregation, consider one of the following:
   - Use stories from the NCM DVDs and *NCM Magazine.*
   - Use Compassionate Connection bulletin inserts (downloadable from the NCM web site).
   - Start a local compassionate ministry center in your community.
   - Start an advocacy group that reads about and acts on social justice issues.

8. Most of all, **pray.** Pray for all those who give a cup of cold water in Christ's name, living compassion as a lifestyle. And pray for those who suffer—for whom acts of compassion are desperately needed.

PRONUNCIATION GUIDE

The following information will assist in pronouncing some unfamiliar words in this book. The suggested pronunciations, though not always precise, are close approximations of the way the terms are pronounced.

Acknowledgments and Prologue

Gustavo Crocker	goo-STAH-voh KRAH-ker
Mhlongo	m-SHLOHN-goh
Siyabonga Kakhulu	see-yah-BOHN-gah kah-KOO-loo
umhawu	oom-HAH-woo

Chapter 1

Ceny Hirahara	SEH-nee hee-rah-HAH-rah
Macungie	muh-KUHN-jee
Sawat Hahom	SAH-WAHT HAH-HOHM
Suvit Amonkulsawat	SOO-VIHT AH-MOHN-KOOL-SAH-WAHT
Thiaw geng	TEE-AW GAYNG
Tomo Hirahara	TOH-moh hee-rah-HAH-rah

Chapter 2

Alfaro	ahl-FAH-roh
Arun Noah	ah-ROON NOH-ah
Dios es Amor	DEE-ohs ehs ah-MOHR
Fernando Melendez	fehr-NAHN-doh meh-LEHN-dehs
Humedica	hoo-MEHD-uh-kah

Iglesia del Nazareno	ee-GLAY-see-ah dehl nah-sah-RAY-noh
Llano Grande	YAH-noh GRAHN-day
Luis Meza	LOO-ees MAY-sah
Santiago Bereche	sahn-tee-AH-goh beh-RAY-chee
Ulyssis Solis	oo-LEE-sees SOH-lees
Uzulutan	oo-zoo-loo-TAHN
Washim	wah-SHEEM

Chapter 3

Anahid	ah-nah-HEED
Akhuryan	ah-koo-ree-AHN
Ara Kodjoyan	AH-rah koh-joh-ee-AHN
Gyumri	GOOM-ree
Habib Alajaji	hah-BEEB ah-lah-JAH-jee
Karen Khachatryan	kah-REEN kah-chah-dree-AHN
Seryan Vardanyan	seh-ree-AHN vahr-dahn-ee-AHN
Yerevan	yehr-uh-VAHN

Chapter 4

Bakasa	bah-KAH-sah
Chikumbi	chee-KOOM-bee
Herrera	eh-REH-rah
Helmer Juárez	EHL-mehr WAH-rehs
Kroeze	KROO-zee
Lasto Mwale	LAS-toh m-WAH-lah
Nyiragongo	NEE-uh-rah-GOHN-goh
Thyolo	CHOH-loh
Trino Jara	TREE-no HAH-rah

Chapter 5

Domasi	doh-MAH-see
Kolapore	KOH-luh-pohr
Wergeland	WERG-luhnd

Chapter 6

Dlamini	dlah-MEE-nee
Hermelinda Toj	ehr-meh-LEEN-dah TOH
Hernesto Toj	ehr-NEHS-toh TOH
Hogar del Niño	oh-GAHR dehl NEEN-yoh
Khulisile (Khuli)	koo-lee-SEE-leh (KOO-lee)
Khumbuzile (Khumbu)	koom-boo-ZEE-leh (KOOM-boo)
Kudakwashe Mudavanhu	koo-dah-KWAH-say moo-dah-VAH-noo
Mantombi	mahn-TOHM-bee
Meo	MAY-oh
Rabinal	rah-bee-NAHL
San Miguel Chicaj	SAHN mee-GEHL chee-KAH

Chapter 7

Arjan	ah-ree-AHN
Astrit	ah-STREET
caj	CHIE
Elmi	ehl-MEE
Fisnik	fihs-NEEK
Ilir	ee-LIHR
Imir Gashi	ee-MIHR GAH-shee
Isuf	ee-SOOF
kos	KOHS
Selim	suh-LEEM
Shirok	shih-ROHK
Shkelzim	shkehl-ZEEM
Ylber	ool-BEHR

Chapter 8

Borgal	BOHR-guhl
El Aposento Alto	ehl ah-poh-SEHN-toh AHL-toh
Prishtina	prish-TEE-nah